SCHOLASTIC

Addition and Subtraction Facts Made Easy

**Ready-to-Use Mini-Lessons and Activities
That Help Students Master Math Facts**

Nicole Iorio

New York • Toronto • London • Auckland • Sydney
Mexico City • New Delhi • Hong Kong • Buenos Aires

Teaching Resources

Editors: Mela Ottaiano, Maria L. Chang
Cover design by Jorge J. Namerow
Interior design by Holly Grundon
SMART™ Notebook files designed and illustrated by Brian LaRossa

ISBN: 978-0-545-19769-4

2 3 4 5 6 7 8 9 10   40   20 19 18 17 16 15 14 13 12

Contents

Addition Strategies

Subtraction Strategies

Introduction

Capturing students' imagination while pushing them to acquire basic skills takes innovation. This book helps you in your quest. It pairs two essential aspects of contemporary math instruction—computation practice and technological tools. *Interactive Whiteboard Activities: Addition and Subtraction Facts Made Easy* features a collection of ready-to-go, interactive mini-lessons and activities that offer students useful strategies and hands-on practice to boost their skills in addition and subtraction.

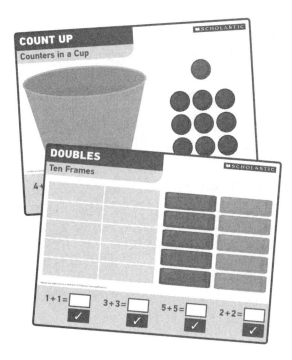

Building Math Fluency

Students are expected not only to be fluent in addition and subtraction facts but also to understand how to solve math problems with reasoning and mathematical thinking. The 15 strategies in this book give students "shortcuts" to help them master their facts quickly, while the 40 interactive whiteboard activities help them apply the strategies to solve math problems and relate them to real-life scenarios.

Each activity in this book provides students with two approaches to solving a problem: First, they learn a mental math strategy that helps them remember particular fact families. Then, they use virtual manipulatives on the interactive whiteboard to confirm their answer. Using both methods gives students an inherent self-checking device and offers you an opportunity to differentiate instruction according to your students' abilities. Regardless of students' level of understanding, they all reach for the same high standards by engaging in these interactive activities that teach them how to apply the math strategies efficiently and effectively, so they feel confident about their knowledge of addition and subtraction facts.

This book features the following essential math strategies:

Addition Strategies

- Count Up (adding 1)
- Two Up (adding 2)
- Doubles (finding the sum of two addends that are the same)
- Neighbors (adding near-doubles)
- Turn Arounds (using the commutative property)
- Ten Again (adding two addends that reach a sum of 10)
- Plus Ten (adding 10)
- Nifty Nine (adding 9)
- Great Eight (adding 8)

Subtraction Strategies

- Back Up (subtracting 1)
- Two Back (subtracting 2)
- Take It All (subtracting a number from itself)
- Take Ten (subtracting 10)
- Nifty Nine (subtracting 9)
- Think Addition (converting a subtraction problem to an addition equation)

Each strategy is presented more than once, using a variety of "virtual" tools on the interactive whiteboard to help reinforce the math concept. To practice the addition strategies, for example, students might manipulate counters in a cup, ten frames, dominoes, and a gumball machine. The subtraction strategies make use of number lines, block towers, beads, and pennies.

As you model how to use these virtual tools, you might also want to provide students with actual hands-on manipulatives—plastic teddy bears, interlocking cubes, beads on strings, coins, and so on—to use at their desks. Other useful tools you may want to offer include number lines, hundreds charts, ten frames, dominoes, addition charts, and subtraction charts.

Enhancing Learning With the Interactive Whiteboard

Why bother using the interactive whiteboard if you already have physical manipulatives on hand? Teaching with the interactive whiteboard has been proven to engage and motivate students—even raise test scores (Marzano and Haystead, 2009). It enhances the way you teach and the way students learn. More and more schools around the country are incorporating the interactive whiteboard into their classrooms as they strive to utilize the latest educational technology. As you've likely already seen, an interactive whiteboard can build bridges in your classroom.

The interactive whiteboard integrates different learning styles. Visual learners are drawn to the colors, numbers, and text on the board, while tactile learners benefit from touching and moving pieces on the board. Math is made easy on the interactive whiteboard, with a variety of ready-made tools students can use as they practice solving math problems. All students become engaged, whether you use the whiteboard in a whole-class or small-group setting, or during individual instruction.

How to Use the Book and CD

The mini-lessons and activities included in the book and companion CD are designed so you can easily incorporate them into your math curriculum. Each mini-lesson in the book includes the following sections:

- **Ready …** An introductory paragraph that tells you what to expect from the activity

- **Set …** A concise explanation of the addition or subtraction strategy students will use

- **Go …** Step-by-step instructions for teaching and modeling the strategy and implementing the activity (provided on the CD) on the interactive whiteboard

- **More Practice** An additional interactive whiteboard activity (also provided on the CD) for further problem-solving practice using the same tools

- **Tech Tips** Suggestions for making the most of the SMART™ Board during your lessons

- **Math Tips** Ways to structure your lessons, as well as suggestions for supporting struggling learners and challenging advanced learners

In addition to the strategy mini-lessons, you will also find instructions on how to use the math templates on the CD to create math problems suited to your students' needs. On the CD, you will also find a matching interactive whiteboard activity for each mini-lesson in the book. Whether you are a novice or an expert interactive whiteboard user, these ready-to-go activities are easy to use. Each one has been created using the SMART Notebook software, ready to use on your SMART Board. Simply pop the CD into your computer and click on the folder to access the interactive whiteboard activities.

> NOTE: You will need the SMART™ Notebook software to open the activities. If you do not have the software, you can go to http://express. smarttech.com and open the Notebook file online or download the free SMART Notebook Express Software onto your computer.

Meeting the Common Core State Standards: Mathematics

The activities in this book and CD help students meet the Standards for Mathematical Practice.

1. Make sense of problems and persevere in solving them.
For each interactive whiteboard activity, students explain the strategy they use and the steps they take to solve each problem. They use tools on the interactive whiteboard to help them solve each addition and subtraction problem and use different methods to check their answers.

2. Reason abstractly and quantitatively.
Students practice responding orally to problems and then demonstrate how to represent them symbolically. They interpret what the quantities mean before they compute.

3. Construct viable arguments and critique the reasoning of others.
Students explain their thinking as they solve problems on the interactive whiteboard, while classmates listen and decide if they agree on the strategy chosen. They are encouraged to ask questions and to offer alternative ideas.

4. Model with mathematics.
Using the math tips, students may connect their computation work to story problems. In this way, they understand situations in which addition and subtraction are used.

5. Use appropriate tools strategically.
Students learn to use the different tools available on the interactive whiteboard to visualize and solve problems, as well as work with traditional manipulatives on their desks as they follow the modeling done on-screen.

6. Attend to precision.
Students use correct mathematical terms as they discuss solutions. They carefully represent each problem with the accurate number of counters.

7. Look for and make use of structure.
Before students begin an interactive whiteboard activity, they may be asked to look for patterns in the problems featured on the board. As a way to understand key concepts, such as the commutative property, they notice how the problems relate to one another.

8. Look for and express regularity in repeated reasoning.
By repeatedly using the same strategy with different on-screen activities, students gain an understanding of concepts that help them master addition and subtraction facts.

The activities in this book and CD also correlate to the following Standards for Mathematical Content.

Operations & Algebraic Thinking
- Represent and solve problems involving addition and subtraction (1.OA, 2.OA)
- Understand and apply properties of operations and the relationship between addition and subtraction (1.OA)
- Add and subtract within 20 (1.OA, 2.OA)
- Work with addition and subtraction equations (1.OA)
- Work with equal groups of objects to gain foundations for multiplication (2.OA)
- Solve problems involving the four operations, and identify and explain patterns in arithmetic (3.OA)

Number and Operations in Base Ten
- Extend the counting sequence (1.NBT)
- Understand place value (1.NBT, 2.NBT)
- Use place value understanding and properties of operations to add and subtract (1.NBT. 2.NBT, 3.NBT)

Measurement and Data
- Work with time and money (2.MD)

Source: Common Core State Standards Initiative
www.corestandards.org/the-standards/mathematics

Count Up: Counters in a Cup

Ready ... Review the Activity

In this activity, students will practice manipulating counters on the interactive whiteboard to solve simple addition problems using the "Count Up" strategy.

Set ... Explain the Strategy

Students use this basic strategy whenever they have to add 1 to any other number. "Counting up" means beginning with the larger number then counting up one number to find the answer.

Go ... Practice the Strategy

1. Display Count Up: Counters in a Cup on the interactive whiteboard. Tell students that they will use the Count Up strategy to solve addition facts that have "+ 1."

2. Demonstrate how to do the first problem: 4 + 1. Drag four blue counters, one at a time, into the cup. Ask: *How many counters do you see in the cup?* (4)

3. Now, move the red counter so that it is just to the side of the cup. Say: *By counting up, all we have to do is think of what comes after 4. That's 5. Now let's use our counters to make sure we're correct.* Touch each of the counters in the cup as you count them and then count the one counter outside of the cup. Tell students that 5 is the correct answer. Write a "5" next to the first problem.

4. Call on student volunteers to solve each of the other problems, following the same simple steps you modeled above. Make sure they pull out the blue counters for the larger number first and drag them into the cup. Then they should drag one red counter to put beside the cup. Next, they should think about counting up. To confirm, they should count the counters inside and outside the cup. Have them write the sum next to the problem.

5. After all the problems have been solved, show students how to check their answers: Simply click on the check boxes below the blank boxes.

TECH TIP:
Smart Pens

When you write the answer to a problem you're modeling, always use the same-color SMART Pen; for example, red. Then when students have their turn, have them use a different-color pen, such as blue, to write their answers.

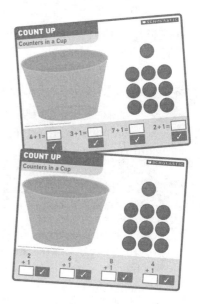

More Practice

Display the second page of Count Up: Counters in a Cup activity. Again, model how to complete the activity (repeat Steps 2 and 3 above). Remind students how they completed the activity with the counters and explain that they will be doing the same exact thing, but with different problems. After students have finished solving the remaining problems, check their answers together.

Count Up: Gumball Machine

Ready ... Review the Activity

In this activity, students will use an old-fashioned gumball machine on the interactive whiteboard to practice the strategy of counting up.

Set ... Explain the Strategy

All the problems in this activity have 1 as an addend. Remind students that they can simply count up one to arrive at the answer.

Go ... Practice the Strategy

1. On the interactive whiteboard, display Count Up: Gumball Machine. Talk with students about what they see on the board: gumball machine with several gumballs and a set of addition problems.

2. Model how to use the gumball machine to help them solve the first problem: 9 + 1. Drag nine green gumballs out of the machine, one at a time. Then drag one blue gumball. (Note that the gumballs are infinitely cloned so you can drag as many gumballs as you need.)

3. Tell students that they'll use the Count Up strategy to find the sum. Say: *I'm going to count 1, 2, 3, 4, 5, 6, 7, 8, and 9. Then 10 comes next.* To confirm your answer, count the number of gumballs outside the machine. After you count the ten gumballs, write "10" as the solution.

4. Now have students try the activity on their own. Invite a volunteer to count the appropriate number of gumballs for each addend and drag them out of the machine. Then have the student count up to find the sum, count all the gumballs again to check, and then write the sum.

5. When all the problems on the board have been solved, check their answers together by clicking on the check boxes.

TECH TIP:
Double Tap

To move something on the board quickly, use two fingers. Put one finger on the item you want to move. Then put a second finger on the new location. Take off your first finger, take off your second finger, and—*voilà!* The item is where you want it.

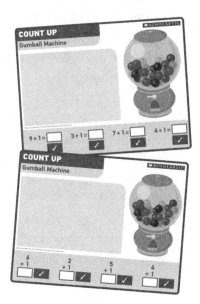

More Practice

Display the second page of Count Up: Gumball Machine on the interactive whiteboard for an extension activity. Students will have more problems to practice adding 1, while playing with gumballs.

Two Up: Counters in a Cup

Ready . . . Review the Activity

In this activity, students practice the Two Up strategy by moving counters to a cup on the interactive whiteboard.

Set . . . Explain the Strategy

With this strategy, students learn to add 2 to any given number by counting up two times from the starting number. As a review, you might want to have students skip-count by 2s, starting with both even and odd numbers.

Go . . . Practice the Strategy

1. Display Two Up: Counters in a Cup on the interactive whiteboard. Ask students which number they will be adding. Confirm that they will be adding 2, and point out how many times "+ 2" appears on the board.

2. Begin with the problem 6 + 2. Tell students that one way to solve it is to think about skip-counting. Say: *I'll count by twos to see what 2 more than 6 is: 2, 4, 6 . . . 8.* Explain that you can stop there since you've gone up 2 from 6.

3. Now point out that you can use counters to find the same answer. Drag six blue counters to the cup, having students count along as you move each counter. Then move two red counters to the side of the cup. Think aloud: *We have six counters in the cup already. We're adding two more. I'll count up from 6. With one more, we have 7. With another, we have 8.* Write "8" as the answer.

4. Invite students to tackle the remaining problems. Let student volunteers take turns dragging counters and writing the sum for each of the remaining problems. Monitor students' work on the board and check their answers when they're done.

MATH TIP:
Steps in Addition Activities

Remind students that even when they know the answer to a problem, like ones with + 2, it helps their brains to learn better when they take the time to first call on a mental math strategy and then manipulate counters to check the sum.

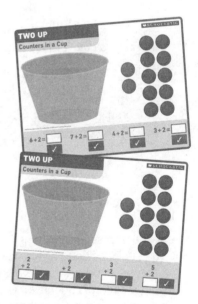

More Practice

Provide students with additional practice with the second page of Two Up: Counters in a Cup activity, using counters to model how to use the Two Up strategy. Show students how to do the first problem, then have them solve the rest. Check their answers together.

Doubles: Counters in a Cup

Ready . . . Review the Activity

Students continue to manipulate counters on the interactive whiteboard to demonstrate how to add doubles.

Set . . . Explain the Strategy

For the Doubles strategy, students count one number twice. Have them think of it as a form of skip-counting. You might also want to explain that this is the basis for multiplication concepts they'll learn later.

Go . . . Practice the Strategy

1. Display Doubles: Counters in a Cup on the interactive whiteboard and ask students what the addition problems have in common. They should notice that in each problem, a number is added to itself. Explain that students will practice adding doubles.

2. Use the first problem as an example: 3 + 3. Drag three red counters over and put them in the cup. Then drag three blue counters in the cup. As you add the three new counters say: *I'll skip-count 3, 6, and stop here to double-check that we now have 6 counters in all in the cup.*

3. Follow up by inviting students to come up to the board and repeat Step 2 to solve the other doubles problems.

4. After you've collaboratively solved the other problems, check their answers by checking on the check boxes.

More Practice

Use the new set of problems from the second page of Doubles: Counters in a Cup to give students more practice with the Doubles strategy. Call on a student volunteer to model the first problem and then three more students to walk through the remaining problems. Each time, have the student say which number he or she will be skip-counting and then count the counters inside the cup to confirm the answers. Check their answers together.

MATH TIP:
Vocabulary of Adding

Take a few minutes to review the words students should know when solving addition problems. Remind them that each *addend* is the number added to reach a *sum*. Students should also be comfortable using *plus, equals, altogether,* and *combine.*

Doubles: Ten Frames

Ready . . . Review the Activity

Students will use a Ten Frame to help them think through addition problems. The Ten Frame is a pictorial model in which students fill boxes with counters to model an addition problem. For this activity, students quickly see that numbers are doubled because each addend takes up an equal number of boxes in the frame.

Set . . . Explain the Strategy

Students will use Ten Frames to add a number to itself. They will also do one-step skip-counting to practice the Doubles strategy. Guide them to notice that the sum of doubles is always an even number.

Go . . . Practice the Strategy

1. Display Doubles: Ten Frames on the interactive whiteboard. Students will quickly notice that in each problem the same number appears twice.

2. Begin with the first problem: 1 + 1. Tell students that you know they can do this problem easily, but you want to show them how a Ten Frame can help in solving addition problems that have the same addends.

3. Model how to move one counter to the bottom left box in the Ten Frame. Say: *This counter stands for the first addend. Now we'll double it by putting another counter in the box next door.* Drag another counter to the bottom right box of the frame.

4. Explain that it's easy to see the problem's solution with the Doubles strategy. Point out that each addend takes up the same amount of space. Count the counters and write "2" as the answer.

5. Invite students to solve the next three problems by dragging counters into the Ten Frame in a symmetrical way so that the concept of doubles is clear. After students have written the sums on the board, check their answers.

TECH TIP:
Screen Shade

The Screen Shade is a useful tool when introducing a lesson. Students can focus on what the problems have in common and which strategy to use. With the Screen Shade, you can hide the Ten Frames or other graphics and counters that appear on the board and show only the problems. Just click the Screen Shade icon on the toolbar to turn it on and off.

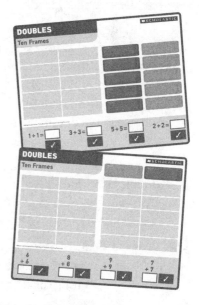

More Practice

Continue the activity on the second page of Doubles: Ten Frames. This time, students will use two Ten Frames. Model how to use a Ten Frame to represent each addend, putting the counters in the same position in each frame. (Note that the counters are infinitely cloned so you can drag as many counters as you need.) Then, add the counters in each Ten Frame together. Invite volunteers to complete the additional problems and review their answers together.

Doubles: Dominoes

Ready ... Review the Activity

Students use pattern cards that look like dominoes on the interactive whiteboard. The number of dots on each side of a domino represents an addend, and students practice adding all the dots to reach a sum.

Set ... Explain the Strategy

Students will practice the Doubles strategy. As they use dominoes with the same number of dots on each side they practice how to skip-count with those various numbers.

Go ... Practice the Strategy

1. Have students share what they know about dominoes. Bring in a set of traditional dominoes, if possible, for students to see and touch as a point of reference.

2. Display Doubles: Dominoes on the interactive whiteboard, and point to the dominoes on the screen. Explain that each domino stands for an addition problem. The number of dots to the left of the line represents the first addend, and the dots on the right side are the second addend.

3. Tell students that they will practice adding doubles. Model the first problem: 5 + 5. Show students how to find the correct domino to represent the problem. Think aloud as you touch each domino that has five dots on the left side. Tell them that for any problem with doubles, the domino should look the same on both sides. When you reach the domino with five dots on each side, drag it to the space above the matching problem.

4. Point out how clear it is to see that the domino is just right for a doubles fact since it is symmetrical, or exactly the same on both sides. Say: *When we add 5 + 5, we get 10. Let's count the dots to check our answer.* After you've counted the dots, write the answer.

5. Invite students to work on the other problems on the board, choosing the appropriate domino for each, recalling the double fact, and then counting the dots to check their answers.

6. Make sure students write the sums to each problem clearly, then click on the check boxes to review their answers.

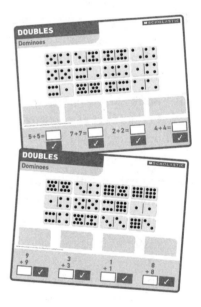

More Practice

Use the second page of Doubles: More Dominoes activity for additional doubles practice. Guide volunteers to complete the activity as you modeled with the first one, and then check the sums together.

Neighbors: Ten Frames

Ready . . . Review the Activity

For this activity, students will use a Ten Frame to help them see that the Neighbors strategy is very similar to Doubles.

Set . . . Explain the Strategy

The addition strategy of Neighbors is a step up from Doubles. One addend is just one number greater than the other addend, making it a "neighbor." As a near-doubles strategy, students can move from Doubles facts to solve Neighbors problems.

Go . . . Practice the Strategy

1. Hold two counters in one hand and two in the other hand. Show both hands to students and remind them that when you add these two sets together, you have a Doubles fact. Next, add another counter to one hand. Explain that adding 3 to 2 is a Neighbors fact. Display Neighbors: Ten Frames on the interactive whiteboard.

2. Think aloud as you walk through the first problem, 3 + 2. Drag three counters to the left column of the Ten Frame. Then drag two counters to the right column. Cover the third counter in the first column so that 2 + 2 is displayed. Say: *If we cover up one counter, we have doubles. Since I see that this problem has just one more than a doubles fact (2 + 2 = 4), I've got my answer just by adding one more.* (5)

3. Count the counters in the Ten Frame to check, then write "5" on the board. Explain that the addition problems on the board are almost like Doubles, but they are called Neighbors instead.

4. Invite student volunteers to come up to solve the other problems on the board. Have them drag the counters into each column of the Ten Frame, count the counters in both columns, and write the sum to each problem.

5. Review and check their answers together by clicking on the check boxes.

More Practice

Display the second page of Neighbors: Ten Frames on the interactive whiteboard. Have students try problems with larger addends, giving them the opportunity to use the two Ten Frames on the board to solve the problems step by step. (Note that the counters are infinitely cloned.) When all the problems have been solved, review the answers together.

MATH TIP:
Small Groups

You may want to call together a small group to work on some addition activities on the interactive whiteboard while the rest of the class works independently or at centers. With just a few students at the board, each student can have a role. For example, one student can talk through the strategy, while two students move the counters for each addend. Another student can use the pen to write the sum, while still another can be in charge of the answer key.

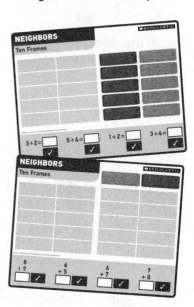

Neighbors: Dominoes

Ready . . . Review the Activity

Students use dominoes to model the Neighbors strategy as they solve addition problems.

Set . . . Explain the Strategy

The Neighbors strategy naturally follows the Doubles strategy. Students solve addition fact problems with addends that are only one digit apart.

Go . . . Practice the Strategy

1. Remind students of the Neighbors strategy and ask them to give examples of addition facts with addends that are Neighbors. Display Neighbors: Dominoes on the interactive whiteboard. Explain to students that they will be using dominoes to help them identify and solve problems that have neighbor numbers.

2. Use the first problem as a model: 6 + 7. Tell students to look through all the dominoes until they find those with six dots on one side. From the dominoes that show six on one side, have students look for one with seven on the other side. Keeping the Neighbors strategy in mind, have students notice that the two sides look almost, but not exactly, alike—one side will have one more dot than the other.

3. When students find the domino with six and seven dots, drag it to the space above the problem. Think aloud: *Using the Doubles strategy, I know that 6 + 6 is 12. So when I see that this problem has one more, I can tell that the sum is 13.*

4. Count all the dots on the domino to check your answer, and then write "13" on the board.

5. With the remaining problems on the board, have students practice choosing the correct dominoes, recalling a related doubles fact, counting, and then solving the problem.

6. Review and check their answers together.

More Practice

Display the second page of Neighbors: Dominoes and challenge students to solve the problems on the board. After you've clicked on the check boxes to confirm all the answers, ask for a volunteer to explain how knowing "neighbors" and using dominoes help with mastering addition facts.

MATH TIP:
Smart Center

Once students have had a chance to work on the addition activities in whole group, small groups, and pairs, they're ready for more independence. Make your SMART Board available during center time. Assign small groups of students to rotate to the board for activities you've selected and displayed on the screen. Guide them to use the SMART tools and to collaborate to solve the problems on the screen. Students should feel at ease with the activities on the board so that you can just stop by to check that they are on task.

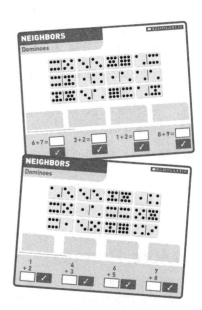

Turn Arounds: Ten Frames

Ready... Review the Activity

The problems for this activity focus on the Turn Arounds strategy (or commutative property), using two Ten Frames as tools to help students visualize the numbers.

Set... Explain the Strategy

The Turn Arounds strategy reminds students that even when the addends in a problem are turned around, the sum remains the same. This is also known as the commutative property.

Go... Practice the Strategy

1. Call out a number of problems and ask students to reply with the correct turn-around pair. For example, when you say, "2 + 5," students should answer, "5 + 2." Then call students' attention to the interactive whiteboard with Turn Arounds: Ten Frames on display.

2. Review how you've used one Ten Frame to show two addends in previous activities. Point out that this time there are two Ten Frames on the board.

3. Model 2 + 5 by moving two counters to the first column of the first Ten Frame. Then drag five counters into the second column of the same frame. (Note that the counters are infinitely cloned.)

4. Next, set up the second Ten Frame for the second problem by reversing what you did in Step 3: Put five counters in the first column and two in the second.

5. Now look at the pair of problems together and ask students what they notice. They should recognize that the frames look flipped from left to right. Ask students what the sum is (7), then call up a student volunteer to check the answer by counting the counters in each Ten Frame. Write the sum on the board.

6. Have students solve the next pair of problems in a similar manner, and then click on the check boxes to confirm.

TECH TIP:
Dragging Objects

Students may have trouble moving counters on the interactive whiteboard. Support them if they lose an object as they're trying to move it. Remind them to keep their finger down as they're dragging something. If they lose contact, the object will stop moving. Tell students that dragging on the SMART Board with a finger is similar to using a mouse on a computer.

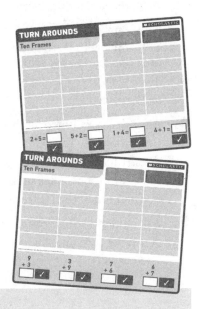

More Practice

Display the second page of Turn Arounds: Ten Frames on the interactive whiteboard and point to the first problem. Ask for volunteers to remind the class how to use two Ten Frames when at least one of the addends in a problem is larger than 5. Guide students to recall from previous activities that a Ten Frame, as its name suggests, can fit only 10 counters. That's why one frame works for addends that are both less than 5. Each addend can then fit in each column. But when an addend is greater than 5, it helps to use one Ten Frame for the first addend and another Ten Frame for the second addend. Proceed with the first pair of problems, challenging students to solve them. When finished, check their answers.

Turn Arounds: Dominoes

Ready . . . Review the Activity

Using on-screen dominoes as visual models for addends, students practice the Turn Arounds strategy with a different set of problems.

Set . . . Explain the Strategy

Students solve addition problems with addends that can be turned around and see that they reach the same answer.

Go . . . Practice the Strategy

1. Display Turn Arounds: Dominoes on the interactive whiteboard. Tell students that they will solve pairs of problems using dominoes to help them.

2. Model choosing appropriate dominoes to represent addends, as you demonstrated in previous activities. Point out that this time, you will only need one domino for two problems because the problems on the board are Turn Arounds.

3. Look at both of the first two problems: 3 + 6 and 6 + 3. Explain that since the addends are simply turned around, the domino you need is the same. Once you've found the domino with three dots on one side and six on the other, remind students that they need to recall only one fact. Say: *I know that 3 + 6 = 9, so that must mean that 6 + 3 also equals 9. To make sure that this answer is correct, let's count the dots on the domino.*

4. After you've counted all the dots, write "9" as the sum for the first two problems. You can rotate the domino to show students that it doesn't matter which number comes first, the total will still be the same. (To rotate, click on the domino so that a box appears around it. Then touch the green circle and drag it around.)

5. Ask students to use one domino to solve the next pair of problems and write the sums. Finish by checking their answers.

More Practice

Have students work on the second page of Turn Arounds: Dominoes for extended practice with the Turn Arounds strategy and dominoes as a model. Review answers together.

TECH TIP:
Digital Ink

When you're writing on the board with a SMART Pen, you are on the digital ink layer. As long as a pen is out of the tray, this layer is available. When you're done working on an activity with students and are ready to either move on to a new screen or complete the lesson, you can use the pop-up menu to choose what to do. You can Save Ink to keep what's on the screen. You can Clear Ink to clear all the writing but keep the digital ink layer. Or you can Close Ink Layer to both clear the writing and close the digital ink layer.

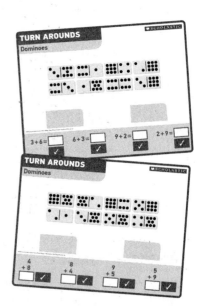

Ten Again: Ten Frames

Ready... Review the Activity

Students will use Ten Frames on the interactive whiteboard to solve problems with two addends that reach a sum of 10.

Set... Explain the Strategy

With the Ten Again strategy, students add pairs of addends to get to 10. Explain to students that they will begin with different numbers and, from there, they will figure out how many more they need to add to reach 10. This strategy also builds subtraction skills.

Go... Practice the Strategy

1. Display Ten Again: Ten Frames on the interactive whiteboard. Ask students to picture how an anchor holds a boat in place. Now have them imagine that 10 is the "anchor" for addition problems. Explain that the problems in this activity are different from past ones because the answer is already clear. The sum is the anchor number, 10. In these problems, students need to figure out the missing addend.

2. Look at the first problem: $7 + \boxed{} = 10$. Remind students that 7 is an addend and 10 is the sum. Point out that solving the problem will begin in the same way as other problems using Ten Frames. Drag seven orange counters to the Ten Frame, filling up the left column with five and the right column with two.

3. Explain to students that they can figure out the missing addend by filling in the empty boxes in the Ten Frame. Drag three green counters to the blank frames. Write "3" on the blank box and say: *We've got the answer we were looking for. We can see that 7 + 3 = 10.*

4. For the next problem, invite a student volunteer to move orange counters for the first addend into the Ten Frame just as you had demonstrated. Then have a second volunteer move green counters for the missing addend. Finish by having the volunteer write the answer on the line and read aloud the complete fact: 4 + 6 = 10.

5. Call up two more volunteers to work through the remaining problems, and then check all their answers together.

MATH TIP:
Pairing Students

Try having a pair of students work together as volunteers to solve all the problems on the interactive board. Have the pair divide up the task of talking through the problem, moving the manipulatives, and writing the answer. In the meantime, the rest of the class can work in pairs at their desks, using hands-on counters and writing on their own small whiteboards, chalkboards, or paper.

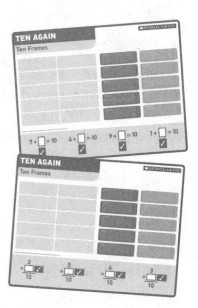

More Practice

Display the second page of Ten Again: Ten Frames. Model the first problem before having students solve the other problems on their own. Review the answers together, then click on the check boxes to confirm their answers.

Ten Again: Dominoes

Ready ... Review the Activity

On the interactive whiteboard, students use dominoes to find addends that add up to 10.

Set ... Explain the Strategy

With the Ten Again strategy, students figure out what number to add to an addend to reach 10. Knowing automatically what pairs of numbers add to 10 will help students later on when they tackle more challenging addition problems.

Go ... Practice the Strategy

1. Display Ten Again: Dominoes on the interactive whiteboard. Tell students that for this activity, their job is to find pairs of numbers that, when added together, equal 10.

2. Model the first problem: *5 +* ☐ *= 10.* Explain to students that you're looking for a missing addend that when added to 5 will give you 10. Ask for students' help to search for dominoes with five dots on one side, then drag the dominoes that meet the criteria to the space above the problem.

3. Next, ask: *Which domino has 10 dots?* (The one with five dots on each side.) Explain to students that you will count aloud how many more dots are on the other side of the domino, counting up from 5: *6, 7, 8, 9, 10.* Say: *We counted five more dots to get to 10. So the answer is 5.* Write "5" on the blank box.

4. Invite student volunteers to come up to the board and follow the steps you modeled to solve the other problems. For each problem, have students fill in the blank with the missing addend. Finish by checking all their answers together.

More Practice

For extended practice with the Ten Again strategy, display the second page of Ten Again: Dominoes on the interactive whiteboard and call on student volunteers to solve the problems. Review the answers together.

TECH TIP:
Pen-Tray Eraser

Remind students that if they make a mistake, it's not a problem. They can erase their writing, just as they do on a regular whiteboard or chalkboard. First, put any pens back in the pen tray. Then have them pick up the eraser to erase anything they've written with a SMART Pen.

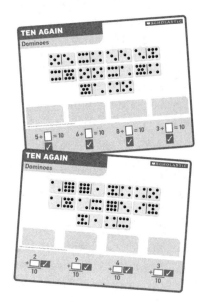

Plus Ten: Dominoes

Ready ... Review the Activity

For this activity, students practice using dominoes to solve problems that have 10 as an addend.

Set ... Explain the Strategy

In an addition problem with 10 as an addend, finding the sum is as simple as adding a 1 to the tens place of the other addend, while keeping the digit in the ones place the same. So, for the problem 10 + 6, simply add a 1 in front of the 6 to get the sum, 16. This is the Plus Ten strategy.

Go ... Practice the Strategy

1. Display a hundred chart. Choose any single-digit number from the top row; for example, 3. Pointing to that number, show students how jumping 10 numbers takes them to the next row, directly below the 3, to the number 13. So 3 + 10 = 13. Do the same with 5 and 8.

2. Explain the Plus Ten strategy to students. If 10 is one of the addends, the sum will have the same number in the ones place as the other addend, but the digit in the tens place will go up by one.

3. Display Plus Ten: Dominoes on the interactive whiteboard. Guide students to notice that each problem has 10 as an addend. Model using the strategy with dominoes. Explain that for this activity, you will use one domino to represent the addend 10 and another domino to stand for the remaining addend.

4. Begin to model the first problem: 7 + 10. First, look for a domino that equals 10 (the one with 5 dots on each side; it is infinitely cloned). Then find a domino that has a total of seven dots (counting both sides). Move the 10 domino to the space above the problem, and then drag over the second domino. Say: *I see that 7 is one of my addends, and there is nothing in the tens place. So when I add 10, I'll just move a 1 to the tens place. So 7 + 10 = 17.*

5. Complete the model problem by counting the number of dots on the two dominoes.

6. Call up volunteers to repeat Steps 4 and 5 with the remaining problems. Check all their answers on the board.

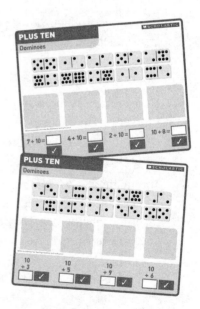

More Practice

For additional practice, have students solve the problems on the second page of Plus Ten: Dominoes. After volunteers have come up to solve the problems, check the answers as a group.

Plus Ten: Gumball Machine

Ready . . . Review the Activity

For this activity, students will use a gumball machine on the interactive whiteboard to help them solve addition problems that has 10 as an addend.

Set . . . Explain the Strategy

Addition problems with 10 as an addend are simple to solve when students remember the Plus Ten rule. The sum will have the same number in the ones place as the other addend that's not 10, while a 1 is added to the tens place (for a single-digit addend).

Go . . . Practice the Strategy

1. Display Plus Ten: Gumball Machine. Ask students to notice what the problems have in common. *(They all have 10 as an addend.)*

2. Demonstrate how to solve the first problem, 10 + 3, using mental math. Say: *I see that this problem has a 10 in it, so I'll use the Plus Ten strategy to help me. That means that I'll look at the other addend, 3. I know that my answer will end in 3. Now I have to make sure that there's nothing in the tens place of that addend. Since there isn't, I can just add a 1 in front of the 3. I get 13.*

3. Now show students how to use the gumball machine to confirm the answer. Drag 10 blue gumballs and then 3 green gumballs from the gumball machine. (Note that the gumballs are infinitely cloned.) Count them. Then write "13" next to the problem.

4. Have student volunteers follow your lead to solve the other problems. They should first use the Plus Ten strategy, and then check their answer using the gumball counters. Finally, have them write the sum.

5. You might also want to remind students of the Turn Arounds strategy. Students should recognize that the sum will always be the same whether the 10 addend comes first or second. Finish by checking answers together.

More Practice

Give students more practice by displaying the second page of Plus Ten: Gumball Machine on the interactive whiteboard. Guide students to complete the problems and then to check their answers.

MATH TIP:
Facts Race

Challenge students to a speed race to show what they know. Take one number-fact strategy they've learned and write several problems that utilize the strategy. Divide the class into two teams. One team can work on the interactive whiteboard, while the other works on chart paper. Give both teams the same set of problems, divided across several screens and pages. Each student can answer four problems and then pass the pen to the next player. The first team to finish—and answer all the problems correctly— wins. Be sure to switch teams between the interactive whiteboard and chart paper after each round.

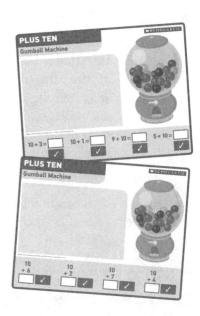

Nifty Nine: Gumball Machine

Ready ... Review the Activity

Students use the gumball machine on this spin-off of the Plus Ten strategy. In this activity, students use the Nifty Nine strategy to solve addition problems with 9 as an addend.

Set ... Explain the Strategy

The concept of adding 9 is easier after students have mastered the Plus Ten strategy. Remind students how adding 10 to a number means adding 1 to the number's tens place. Explain that once they know this, they just need to count back one to use the Nifty Nine strategy.

Go ... Practice the Strategy

1. Display Nifty Nine: Gumball Machine on the interactive whiteboard. Ask students what the problems have in common. (*They all have 9 as an addend.*)

2. Model how to solve the first problem: 2 + 9. Explain that first, you'll do mental math, similar to how you use the Plus Ten strategy. That is, you'll think 10 more and arrive at the sum by adding a 1 in front of the addend 2. That would make 12.

3. Now explain that there's one more step in the Nifty Nine strategy. Say: *We know 12 is the answer to 2 + 10. And we know that 9 is one less than 10. So we'll just drop back one from 12 to get to 11. That is the sum: 2 + 9 = 11.*

4. Confirm the sum by counting gumballs. Drag two blue gumballs from the machine and then drag nine green gumballs. Count how many gumballs there are in all. Once you've counted the total (*11*), write the answer on the board.

5. Invite students to test out the Nifty Nine strategy by using the gumball machine. They should follow the same order of steps you modeled. Also, have students recall the Turn Arounds strategy (or commutative property), noting that the order of addends doesn't matter.

6. When all the problems on the board have been solved, check their answers by clicking on the check boxes.

TECH TIP:
Orienting

You may sometimes notice that your marks don't show up exactly where you want them on the board. You might need to reorient the SMART Board. To correct the alignment, press and hold the keyboard and right mouse buttons at the same time. When the Orientation screen appears, follow the steps and touch the diamond icons to reorient the screen.

More Practice

For more practice with the Nifty Nine strategy using the gumball machine, have students work on the second page of Nifty Nine: Gumball Machine. Check all the answers on the board.

Great Eight: Gumball Machine

Ready ... Review the Activity

Using a gumball machine on the interactive whiteboard to represent addends and the sum, students will practice the Great Eight strategy.

Set ... Explain the Strategy

Expanding on the strategies Plus Ten (adding 10 to a number) and Nifty Nine (adding 9 to a number), students will use a similar mental math strategy to add 8. The Great Eight strategy starts out the same way as Nifty Nine in that you picture what the sum of the problem would be if 10 were added. This time, however, students count back two numbers from 10.

Go ... Practice the Strategy

1. Ask for volunteers to describe how the Plus Ten and Nifty Nine strategies work. Then tell the class that you'll show another similar strategy, called Great Eight. This time, the addition problems will all have 8 as an addend.

2. Display Great Eight: Gumball Machine on the interactive whiteboard. Explain that you'll do mental math first and then check your answer by counting the gumballs you've taken out of the machine.

3. Use the first problem as an example. Say: *Let's look at 8 + 5. I see that 8 is one of the addends, so that tells me I can use Great Eight. But first, I'll think of Plus Ten. So instead of adding 8 and 5, I'll add 10 and 5. I know that when I add 10 to a number less than 10, I only need to add 1 to the number's tens place, so the sum of 10 + 5 is 15.*

4. Next, tell students that to find the sum of 8 + 5, they'll need to count back 2, because 8 is 2 less than 10. Think aloud: *When we count back 2 from 15, we get 14, then 13. So 13 is the sum of 8 and 5.*

5. Tell students that you'll use gumballs to check your answer. Move eight green gumballs from the machine. Then drag out five blue gumballs. Count all the gumballs you now have, and write "13" as the answer.

6. Have students practice solving problems with 8 as an addend, following the same steps you've modeled. Check answers together.

MATH TIP:
RTI and Building on Basic Facts

Give students a chance to recall what they know before beginning an interactive whiteboard lesson or moving on to More Practice. Take a strategy like Great Eight and work with a small group of students to have them recite their math facts (as in 8 + 1, 8 + 2, 8 + 3, and so on). Point out that memorizing and retrieving facts automatically will help them in solving more advanced math problems. Using counters and other manipulatives to show their work also helps solidify their knowledge.

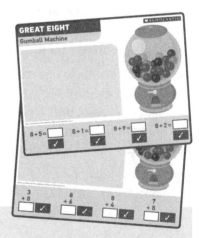

More Practice

Use the second page of Great Eight: Gumball Machine to give students more practice with the Great Eight strategy. Review sums by counting gumballs. As students solve these problems, remind them that the order of the addends won't affect the strategy, just as they learned from Turn Arounds. That means that Great Eight works whether 8 is the first addend or the second.

Addition Template: Counters in a Cup

Ready ... Review the Activity

After students have had practice moving counters into and out of a cup to help them understand various addition strategies, you can create your own counters-in-a-cup activity using the sample basic setup.

Set ... Explain the Strategy

Use Counters in a Cup to give students additional practice in any strategy they still need to master or to introduce another addition strategy.

Go ... Practice the Strategy

1. First, decide on the strategy you want to use. On the board, write a set of addition problems that utilize that strategy. You may wish to do this before students arrive, or you can think aloud as you write the problems.

2. Display Addition Template: Counters in a Cup on the interactive whiteboard for students to see. Explain which strategy students will be using and any tips you want to remind them about.

3. Call on various students and have them take turns solving the problems. Encourage them to use the counters to confirm their answers. (Note that the counters are infinitely cloned.)

4. Review their answers together.

More Practice

If you want to extend practice for your students, just erase the problems and answers you've written up. Write another set of problems in the same space. You can delete the counters you've already used. Then, have students solve the new set of problems. Repeat as often as you like, given the needs and interests of your class.

TECH TIP:
Writing Clearly

Make sure that students know how to hold the SMART Pen to the screen so that their printing is clear. If students are making up their own problems, make sure their numbers appear legibly or their friends may not be able to solve them! Remind them to apply solid pressure with the pen, making sure their hand is not in the way. It may take some practice to write right!

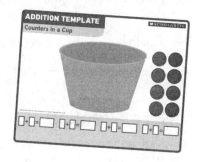

Addition Template: Ten Frames

Ready... Review the Activity

Once students are familiar with how Ten Frames work, they are ready for more practice using these pictorial models. You can choose the type of addition problems you want students to practice.

Set... Explain the Strategy

You pick the strategy, and you create the addition problems. Based on what you've seen from your students work, you may wish to emphasize a strategy with which they have struggled or provide problems using a mix of strategies previously introduced for use with Ten Frames.

Go... Practice the Strategy

1. Write addition problems, and then review with students what you expect them to do.

2. Display the Addition Template: Ten Frames on the interactive whiteboard. Review and model how to use the Ten Frame first, if necessary, then let students start solving the problems.

3. Provide guidance about using one or two Ten Frames, as needed. (Note that the Ten Frame and the counters are infinitely cloned.)

4. Finally, check their answers together.

TECH TIP:
Digital Pen

Don't forget that the handheld SMART Pens aren't the only way to write on the SMART Board. If it's not already up, launch Floating Tools and click on the Digital Pen icon. This tool allows you to write with your finger instead of a pen. You can also choose from a variety of ink colors.

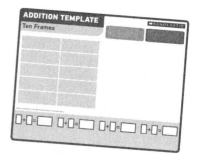

More Practice

Provide another set of problems if any students need additional practice. If you used one Ten Frame for the first set of problems, try using two Ten Frames the second time. Have students work together, and then check their answers.

Addition Template: Dominoes

Ready... Review the Activity

Use this template to create your own dominoes and addition problems to extend students' practice.

Set... Explain the Strategy

Review any of the addition strategies that use dominoes, then write your own addition problems and allow students to use these manipulatives to check their answers.

Go... Practice the Strategy

1. Offer more practice by deciding which strategy students most need to work on and setting up the board as will serve them best. Using the Addition Template: Dominoes, write the problems first and then create dominoes that match the addends, making sure to include incorrect options. (Note that the blank dominoes are infinitely cloned. You can drag as many dominoes as you need. To create the spots, select the black SMART Pen, then click on Properties. Click on Line Style, select a heavy line under Thickness, then put any number of dots on the domino.)

2. Display the Addition Template: Dominoes, featuring your own addition problems on the interactive whiteboard. Go over directions with students.

3. Challenge students to solve the problems on the board, and then review the answers together.

TECH TIP:
Magic Pen

Give students a chance to play teacher with practice boards you create, based on templates like the one on this page. Show students how to circle text—a problem, an addend, or a sum—using the Magic Pen on the board. This gesture will make the rest of the board darken momentarily as a spotlight brings focus to the circled portion. It's a fun way for one student to point something out to a peer.

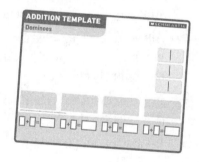

More Practice

If more practice seems like a good idea, erase the problems you've written and the dominoes you've created. Vary the activity by working on a different strategy or giving students a mix of addition problems. Write more problems for students to solve, and make corresponding dominoes.

Addition Template: Gumball Machine

Ready . . . Review the Activity

Motivate students to practice more addition problems using the gumball machine. Offer more problems with this template.

Set . . . Explain the Strategy

Review any addition strategy or set of strategies by writing problems for the gumball-machine template.

Go . . . Practice the Strategy

1. Decide on the addition problems you want to give students, and write them on Addition Template: Gumball Machine on the interactive whiteboard.

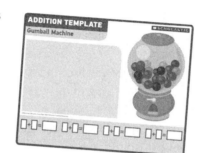

2. Discuss what you want students to get out of the activity, emphasizing the strategy or strategies they should practice.

3. Allow students to solve the problems on the board, using the gumball machine to check their answers. (Note that the gumballs are infinitely cloned.)

4. Invite students to write problems for their peers, suggesting which strategy they should use.

5. Review the problems and their answers as a group.

More Practice

Remember that you can erase the problems you've just used. Write additional problems that suit your students. Have students solve them, and then check their answers.

TECH TIP:
Floating Toolbar

Launch the Floating Toolbar to see your tool options other than those on the pen tray. Just as the Digital Pen is valuable on the template boards, so is the Digital Eraser. Let students take turns using it to erase problems they've written on the board as they prepare to write another set. Point out that they can also change the size of the eraser.

Pointer With the pointer, students can focus on a particular part of the screen.

Calculator If you want, show students how to use the calculator as another way of checking answers or trying out a series of problems that fit the strategy you're using.

As an alternative to writing, you can type with the on-screen keyboard. You may wish to use this to type in story problems related to the math facts you're working on.

Recorder Use the recorder to record what you do on the board. This could be useful if you want to talk through steps for demonstrating a strategy. You can even add audio and video.

Back Up: Number Line

Ready ... Review the Activity

Using a number line on the interactive whiteboard, students will subtract 1 from numbers 1 to 9.

Set ... Explain the Strategy

Subtracting 1 from any number is easy when students remember the Back Up strategy. They simply "back up" one tick mark on the number line or count back by one.

Go ... Practice the Strategy

1. Display Back Up: Number Line on the interactive whiteboard. Ask students to recall how a number line helps them add or subtract numbers. Explain that in a number line, each number is represented by a tick mark on the line. Note that this number line starts at 0 and continues up to 10. To add to a number, simply "hop" to the right; to subtract, hop to the left.

2. Ask students what they notice about the problems in this activity. (*They all involve "– 1."*) Explain that the Back Up strategy is useful for this kind of subtraction facts. Tell students that whenever they see a subtraction problem with "– 1," all they have to do is back up one from the larger number. The number line helps them see how to back up by hopping backward by one.

3. Model how to use the number line for the first problem: 3 – 1. Position the SMART Pen on the 3 on the number line. Then, bounce the pen in a half-circle to go back one on the number line, landing at 2. Write "2" as the answer to the first problem.

4. Encourage students to practice the activity on their own. Call on a student volunteer to use the SMART Pen to Back Up one to solve the next problem and to write the difference. Invite more volunteers to solve the remaining problems.

5. Ask a volunteer to remind the class why the strategy is called Back Up and how the number line helps show this strategy. Finish up by checking the answers together.

More Practice

For more practice in subtracting 1, go to the second page of Back Up: Number Line. Call on a student to lead this extension activity. The student should read the first problem aloud, explain what to do to solve it, use the pen on the number line and write the answer. Let the student call on additional volunteers. Have the student leader be in charge of checking answers for the board.

Language of Subtraction

Help students remember the parts of a subtraction problem. The first number (or the top number) in a subtraction problem is called the *minuend*. This number tells the amount from which another amount is subtracted. The number that tells how much to subtract is called the *subtrahend*. This number is the second number (or the bottom number) of a subtraction problem. The solution to a subtraction problem is called the *difference*. Students should also know the terms *minus*, *take away*, *fewer*, *less than*, and *equals*. Create bingo boards with addition and subtraction words as a playful way to build students' math vocabulary.

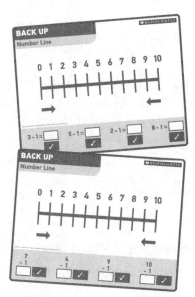

Back Up: Block Towers

Ready . . . Review the Activity

This activity gives students more practice with the Back Up strategy. Students will build towers using virtual blocks on the interactive whiteboard.

Set . . . Explain the Strategy

Back Up is a strategy students can use when they see 1 as the subtrahend. What they need to remember is very basic: back up one from the minuend.

Go . . . Practice the Strategy

1. Display Back Up: Block Towers on the interactive whiteboard. Tell students that they'll be building towers to model subtracting 1.

2. Ask students if they remember what subtraction strategy can help them solve the problems they see on the board. Guide them to notice the "– 1" in each problem and to recall the Back Up strategy. Tell students that you'll think about the math in your head first and then use blocks on the board for building.

3. Walk through the first problem: 8 – 1. Say: *In my head, I'll think about what I do when I count backwards. I'll start at 8 since that's the minuend. Going back one, I get to 7. Now I'll build a tower to see if I can show the answer another way.*

4. Drag eight blocks from the side of the screen, counting aloud as you move each one. (Note that the blocks are infinitely cloned so you can drag as many blocks as you need.) Assemble the eight blocks into a tower. Say: *So we start with 8 blocks. Now I'll take one block away to show – 1.* Take the top block from the tower and put it right next to it. Ask: *How many blocks are left?* Count the remaining blocks and write the answer "7" next to the first problem.

5. Invite students one at a time to solve a problem on the board using the Back Up strategy and building a tower. As they work at the board, ask them to explain what they're doing out loud.

6. Remind students of the two ways they're solving these subtraction problems: in their heads with the Back Up strategy and by building blocks. Click on the check boxes to confirm their answers.

TECH TIP:
Printing With SMART Notebook

You may want to print some of the activities you're using on the SMART Board for students to use as independent practice at their desks, for homework assignments, or for students who were absent when you taught a lesson. Go to File, then Print, and you'll find the options to print Thumbnails, Handouts, and Full Page. When you print Full Page, students can see the whole Notebook slide as the class sees it on the SMART Board.

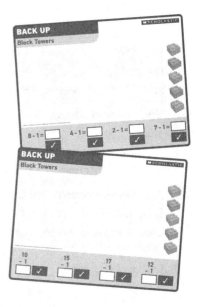

More Practice

Go to the second page of Back Up: Block Towers to give students more practice with subtracting 1.

Back Up: Pockets

Ready . . . Review the Activity

Students work with pockets and coins on the interactive whiteboard to solve subtraction problems. They practice subtracting one penny from two or more pennies.

Set . . . Explain the Strategy

To use the Back Up strategy, students subtract 1 from any number and think of it as counting back one.

Go . . . Practice the Strategy

1. Tell students that they will be playing with money on the interactive whiteboard. Each penny on the board represents the number 1.

2. Display Back Up: Pockets on the board and ask students what number gets subtracted in each problem they see. *(1)* Ask: *What strategy do we use when we subtract 1?* (Back Up)

3. Using the first problem, 5 – 1, model how the pennies and pockets represent the parts of the subtraction problem. Say: *First, I'll use the Back Up strategy to figure out the answer. I'll just back up one from 5, which brings me to 4. Now, I'll use the pennies and pockets to check.*

4. Drag five pennies into the left pocket, explaining that this pocket represents the minuend in the problem. Next, move one penny from the first pocket into the second pocket. Explain that this represents the subtrahend. Ask: *How many are left in the first pocket?* Count together, then write "4" next to the first problem.

5. Invite students to come up to the board and solve the other problems the same way you did: first by using the Back Up strategy to find the solution, and then by moving pennies into pockets to show how they got the answer. When students have finished, have them write their answer next to each problem.

6. Finish the activity by clicking on the check boxes to confirm answers.

More Practice

Go to the second page of the Back Up: Pockets activity. Guide volunteers to complete the activity in the same way you've modeled. Then check the differences together.

MATH TIP:
Pocket Practice

Invite students to bring in collections of small items, such as pebbles, buttons, erasers, and acorns. Bring in an apron that has pockets or ask families for donations of used clothing with pockets. Let students work with a partner or small group at a center, using their collections as manipulatives to put into and take out of pockets. Have one child say or write a problem for another child. Then have the other child practice putting the correct number of items into each pocket to arrive at the correct sum or difference.

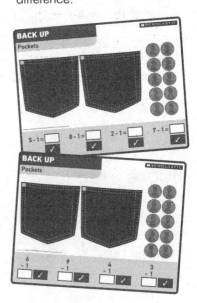

Two Back: Number Line

Ready . . . Review the Activity

Students build on what they know about using number lines for subtraction and hopping back. For this activity, they use the Two Back strategy to solve subtraction problems.

Set . . . Explain the Strategy

The Two Back strategy is the next natural step after students have practiced the Back Up strategy. Rather than counting back one to subtract, problems with 2 as the subtrahend require going Two Back.

Go . . . Practice the Strategy

1. Display Two Back: Number Line on the interactive whiteboard. Ask students what number they see in every subtraction problem on the board. (2)

2. Tell students that when they see a problem with 2 as the subtrahend, they can use the Two Back strategy. Just as the strategy name says, this means counting back two.

3. Use the first problem, $8 - 2$, to show students how to count back two on a number line. Say: *I see that we start with 8, so I'll put the pen on the 8 on the number line. Now we've got to count back two. So let's hop back once to 7 and then a second time to 6. That means $8 - 2 = 6$.* Write "6" as the answer to the first problem.

4. Invite students to solve the remaining problems using the Two Back strategy. Remind them to use the number line before writing the answer, even if they can solve the problem in their heads.

5. Check all the answers at the same time.

More Practice

Give students more practice using the number line with the Two Back strategy. Display the second page of Two Back: Number Line on the board and ask volunteers to complete the problems. Then check their answers together.

Pointer

TECH TIP: SMART Pointer

The pointer function of the SMART Board works in the same way as a traditional pointer. To access the pointer, press the SMART Board icon at the bottom right of your screen and call up the Tools menu. Click on Other Tools > Pointer. Then you can use the arrow to point out the number you want to hop to on the number line, or the minuend, subtrahend, or anything else on the board you want students to focus on. When possible, give students a chance to use the pointer as well.

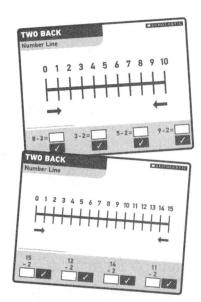

Two Back: Block Towers

Ready ... Review the Activity

When students use block towers to model subtraction problems, they will understand that subtracting 2 is very similar to backing up twice.

Set ... Explain the Strategy

The Two Back strategy involves counting back from the minuend two times. This strategy is used for any problem in which 2 is subtracted from a number.

Go ... Practice the Strategy

1. Ask students if they can remember a subtraction strategy for problems with "– 2." Tell them that for today's lesson, they will practice counting back two with the Two Back strategy and then build block towers on the interactive whiteboard to check their answers.

2. Display Two Back: Block Towers on the interactive whiteboard. Using your finger or pointer, touch the 2 on each problem. Remind students that the second or bottom number in a subtraction problem is called the *subtrahend*.

3. Work through the first problem: 6 – 2. Say: *Let's count back 2 from 6. We start with 6 and count back—5, 4. Then we stop there. So our answer is 4. Now we'll build a tower to check.*

4. Drag blocks from the side of the screen to build a tower with a height of six. (Note that the blocks are infinitely cloned.) Ask: *How many blocks do you see?* (6) *How many will be left when we take two away?* (4) Demonstrate, then write "4" as the answer.

5. Call on student volunteers to solve the remaining problems using the Two Back strategy and then confirm their answers using the blocks. Click on the check boxes to confirm their answers.

More Practice

Give students extended practice with subtracting 2. Display the second page of Two Back: Block Towers on the interactive whiteboard and choose different volunteers to lead the problem solving on the board.

MATH TIP:
Fact Families

Have students complete sets of related problems to help them develop fluency with fact families. Guide students to see the connection between addition and subtraction by writing various subtraction problems on a blank SMART Notebook page. Explain to students that they can rethink these subtraction problems as addition problems with missing addends. For example, 6 – 2 = ___ is the same as 2 + ___ = 6. Then ask them to think of other related facts; in this case, 6 – 4 = 2 and 4 + 2 = 6.

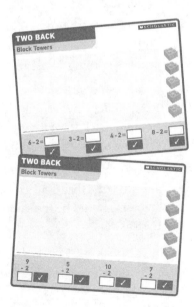

Take It All: Number Line

Ready . . . Review the Activity

Students will use the number line on the interactive whiteboard to show subtraction facts that require taking the number from itself.

Set . . . Explain the Strategy

Take It All means to subtract a number from itself. Students will understand that when all is taken away, nothing is left, and so the answer to any of these problems is zero.

Go . . . Practice the Strategy

1. Display Take It All: Number Line on the interactive whiteboard. Ask students what they notice about the problems on the board. They should quickly see that in all the problems, the minuend and subtrahend are the same numbers.

2. Tell students that there's an easy way to remember subtraction facts that have the same minuend and subtrahend. The strategy is called Take It All because the problem asks that everything be taken away.

3. Say: *Let's look at the first problem, 10 – 10. I know the answer to this problem right away when I recall the Take It Away strategy.* (Hold up all 10 of your fingers.) *When I take 10 from 10, there's nothing left.* (Put down all 10 fingers.) *But I can use the number line to confirm. Watch as I count back 10 from 10.*

4. Use the SMART Pen to hop back 10 tick marks from the number 10 on the number line. Point out that you ended up at 0, which is the same as nothing. Write the answer "0" next to the problem.

5. Invite a student volunteer to practice thinking through the Take It All strategy by reading aloud the next problem on the board, hopping back the appropriate number of marks, and writing the difference next to the problem. Call on other volunteers to repeat with the remaining problems.

6. Tell students that if they've used the strategy correctly, then all the answers should be the same: 0. Click on the check boxes to confirm the answers.

More Practice

Go to the second page of Take It All: Number Line to have students try out the number line as a model for more basic subtraction facts. Check answers together.

MATH TIP:
Give and Take

For younger students, the concept of Take It All will best register when they can see that there is something at the start of the problem and nothing left at the end. Provide them with hands-on manipulatives to use as you and student volunteers work on the whiteboard. Set aside 20 counters for each pair of students. Have one student count and place the correct number of counters on the table to represent the minuend. Then have the partner take away the counters one at a time as they watch that amount being counted back on the number line. Invite partners to switch roles.

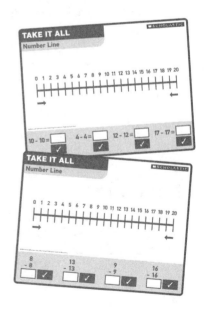

Take It All: Beads

Ready ... Review the Activity

Students manipulate beads on the interactive whiteboard to work through subtraction problems that have the same number for the minuend and subtrahend.

Set ... Explain the Strategy

For this strategy, students solve problems in which everything is taken away. The answer is always 0.

Go ... Practice the Strategy

1. Display Take It All: Beads on the interactive whiteboard. Point out that there are a lot of double numbers on the subtraction problems on the board. Ask if anyone knows which strategy will help.

2. Tell students to imagine that they're making bead necklaces but then change their minds. Think aloud as you solve the first problem: 7 – 7. Say: *I'm going to pick out some beautiful beads to make a necklace. Here's a purple one, a blue one, a green one, an orange one, a pink one, another purple one, another blue one, and one more, a green one. We have seven beads.* (Note that the beads are infinitely cloned so you can drag as many beads so you need.) *Hmmm. I don't like this necklace. I'm going to take all the beads away.* Count back from 7 to 1 as you remove each bead, one at a time, from the necklace.

3. Show that the necklace is now empty. Explain that when you take 7 away from 7, there is nothing left. Write "0" as the answer.

4. Call on volunteers to act out the necklace building and taking apart, as you've modeled.

5. Reiterate that whenever a subtraction problem has the same number for both the minuend and subtrahend, the answer will always be zero. Check students' answers on the board.

More Practice

Have students solve similar problems using beads on the second page of Take It All: Beads. They will see that regardless of the problem, the answer is always zero when the two numbers in the subtraction problem are the same.

Magnifier

TECH TIP: SMART Magnifier

If you or any students have trouble seeing something on the SMART Board, or if you want to enlarge a number for emphasis, use the magnifier tool. Two windows appear when you click on the magnifier. The smaller window lets you choose what you want to magnify and the larger window displays the enlarged view.

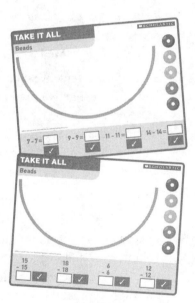

Take Ten: Number Line

Ready . . . Review the Activity

This activity gives students practice in subtracting 10 using a number line.

Set . . . Explain the Strategy

In the Plus Ten addition strategy, students learned that it's easy to add 10 to a number since the digit in the ones place of the number being added to doesn't change. The same concept applies in Take Ten—whenever 10 is the subtrahend in a math fact from 10 to 19, the difference is simply the number in the ones place of the minuend. For example, in 16 – 10, the minuend is 16, so the difference will be 6.

Go . . . Practice the Strategy

1. Tell students that you're going to practice subtracting 10 by calling on the Take Ten strategy. Show students how to do this on the hundred chart by putting your finger on a number; for example, 13. Say: *Let's subtract 10 from 13. The hundred chart makes it clear. We just go up one space and land on the box in the row above to get our answer of 3. Notice that the answer is simply the digit in the ones place. That is always true when we Take Ten.*

2. Turn to the interactive whiteboard and show students the number line on Take Ten: Number Line. Explain that you can use a number line to get the same result as you did on the hundred chart. Starting from 13, draw 10 hops as half-circles from 9 to 8 to 7 and so on. As you use the pen to hop from 4, draw an arrow pointing to the final number, 3.

3. Read aloud the complete subtraction fact as you write the answer: *13 – 10 = 3.*

4. Erase your writing above the number line, and ask student volunteers to follow the steps you modeled to solve the remaining problems. Have each volunteer talk through the 10 hops while drawing them on the whiteboard. After each problem has been solved and its answer written, click on its check box.

Highlighter

TECH TIP: SMART Highlighter

Call up the SMART Tools menu to use the Highlighter tool. In math activities, you may find the Highlighter to be a helpful tool when you first open the board and ask students to notice what the problems have in common. You may want to highlight each subtrahend to show a pattern, or you can call up a volunteer to do this. Highlight any area in your choice of color.

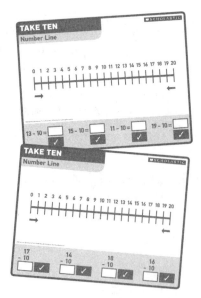

More Practice

Encourage students to practice hopping back on a number line with the second page of Take Ten: Number Line.

Take Ten: Beads

Ready . . . Review the Activity

On the interactive whiteboard, students practice the Take Ten strategy by moving various numbers of beads onto a necklace and then taking 10 away.

Set . . . Explain the Strategy

Take Ten is the strategy used for subtracting 10 from any number. The trick for students to remember is that the answer has the same digit in the ones place as the minuend.

Go . . . Practice the Strategy

1. Let students know that they'll be working with beads in sets of ten for the problems in this activity. Display Take Ten: Beads. Note that the subtrahend in each problem is 10.

2. Model the first problem: 16 – 10. Remind students of the Take Ten strategy. Say: *When I take 10 away from a number, I remember to keep the ones place the same and look at the tens place. Starting with 16, that means I drop the 1 in the tens place and keep the ones place as is. So we're left with 6.*

3. Follow up by using beads to demonstrate the problem. Drag 16 beads onto the necklace, counting aloud as you do. (Note that the beads are infinitely cloned.) Then drag 10 of them off. Ask: *How many beads are left?* (6) Count the remaining beads and write the answer next to the problem.

4. Invite students to take a turn on the board. Encourage them to solve the remaining problems using Take Ten and by counting beads.

5. Confirm that their answers are correct by clicking on the check boxes.

More Practice

Give students time to solidify their understanding of the Take Ten strategy as they play with on-screen beads. Use the second page of Take Ten: Beads.

MATH TIP: Regular Routines

Incorporate addition and subtraction strategies into your daily routines. For example, have students practice working with numbers in sets of ten as you distribute papers and other materials. You can give out ten copies to a student volunteer and ask how many more you need so that all the students in the class have a copy. Or you can ask ten students to line up and then have the class figure out how many students are left. You can also practice telling time in ten-minute intervals by estimating the number of minutes left on the clock until lunchtime.

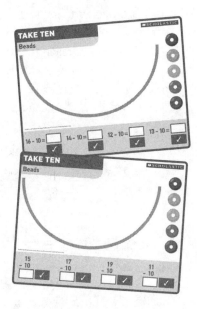

Take Ten: Pockets

Ready ... Review the Activity

On the interactive whiteboard, students move pennies into pockets to demonstrate the Take Ten strategy for subtraction.

Set ... Explain the Strategy

When students take 10 away from numbers 10 to 19, they will discover that the answer is simply the number in the ones place of the minuend.

Go ... Practice the Strategy

1. Display Take Ten: Pockets on the interactive whiteboard and tell students that they'll practice the Take Ten strategy using pennies on the board.

2. Model the first problem: 12 – 10. Say: *First, I'll take 10 away in my mind. If I hop back 10, I'll wind up with 2 since I know that the answer is the same as the number in the ones place of the minuend. Then I'll use pennies as counters to check.*

3. Explain that another way to look at the problem is to think that the total number of pennies we have is 12. Imagine that only 10 of those pennies can fit in one pocket. Ask: *How many more pennies do we need to add to the other pocket to get 12 pennies in all?*

4. Drag ten pennies one-by-one into the left pocket, counting as you move them. Then explain that you'll be putting pennies into the second pocket to get to 12. Instead of counting from 1, you'll start from 11, since there already are 10 pennies in the other pocket, and stop when you reach the total, 12. Count aloud as you drag pennies into the right pocket: *11, 12.* To find out how many more pennies you needed to get to 12, count the pennies in the second pocket. Then write "2" as the answer to the first problem.

5. Have students solve the remaining problems using the Take Ten strategy and putting pennies into pockets. Then ask a volunteer to click on the check boxes on the board.

More Practice

Give students additional practice subtracting ten pennies from other numbers. Go to the second page of Take Ten: Pockets. Work collaboratively with the on-screen counters and the subtraction strategy.

Calculator

TECH TIP:
SMART Calculator

Students may enjoy checking their answers by using the SMART Calculator tool. From SMART Tools, click on the icon that looks like a traditional hand-held calculator. Show students where to find the minus, plus, and equal keys. The calculator is also useful if you want to give students additional problems that connect to the strategy you're using.

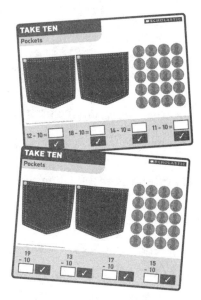

Nifty Nine: Block Towers

Ready... Review the Activity

On the interactive whiteboard, students build a tower of blocks to help solve subtraction problems in which 9 is the subtrahend.

Set ... Explain the Strategy

Students take their knowledge of Take Ten and adapt it to the Nifty Nine strategy. In subtraction problems where the subtrahend is 9, students first think of the Take Ten strategy to drop to the digit in the minuend's ones place. Then, remembering that 10 is one more than 9, they go up one to get the final answer.

Go ... Practice the Strategy

1. On the interactive whiteboard, display Nifty Nine: Block Towers. Ask students what number they see in every problem on the board. (9) Explain that for problems in which 9 is subtracted, the Nifty Nine strategy comes in handy.

2. Model with the first problem: 14 – 9. Explain to students that first you're going to think it through in your head, and afterward, you'll use blocks to check the answer. Tell students to pretend that the subtrahend is 10 instead of 9. Say: *I know that if we go back 10, we end at 4 since the Take Ten rule says that we keep the number in the ones place. But the subtrahend is 9 instead of 10. Nine is one number away from 10. So instead of going all the way back to 4, we stop at one number away: 5.*

3. Next, demonstrate how to use blocks to check your answer. Tell students that you'll build a tower, which will have the number of blocks in the minuend. Drag 14 blocks from the side of the screen and assemble them into a tower. (Note that the blocks are infinitely cloned.) Say: *Let's see how many blocks will remain if we take away 9.* Drag nine blocks from the top of the tower and put them to one side. Ask: *How many blocks are left?* (5) Write the answer next to the first problem.

4. Give students a turn at block building. Make sure to clear all the blocks after each turn. (You can delete the blocks.) Then, as each volunteer comes up, remind the student to first think through the Nifty Nine strategy before dragging blocks into a tower.

5. Click on the check boxes to confirm their answers together.

MATH TIP:
Interlocking Cubes

Provide students with interlocking cubes so they can work along with you as they sit on the rug or at their desks by using their own sets of interlocking cubes. As you model the first problem on the interactive whiteboard for Block Towers, have students snap together the same number of blocks you're using and display their towers. Ask them to continue building their own towers as you call up volunteers to work on the board.

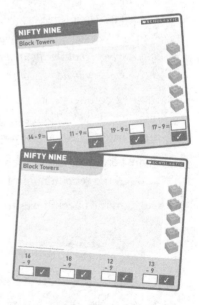

More Practice

Display the second page of Nifty Nine: Block Towers to give students more practice in subtracting 9. Ask different volunteers to come up to the board and think aloud each step as they solve the problem. Check answers together.

Nifty Nine: Beads

Ready . . . Review the Activity

In this activity, students make bead necklaces, then take nine beads from each one to represent different subtraction problems with 9 as the subtrahend.

Set . . . Explain the Strategy

As its name suggests, the Nifty Nine strategy for subtraction is used for problems that have 9 as the subtrahend. Since 9 is only one number away from 10, students can start by using the Take Ten strategy to think about what the difference would be if 10 were subtracted from the minuend. Then, since 10 is one number up from 9, they go up one number to get the difference for – 9.

Go . . . Practice the Strategy

1. Remind students that Nifty Nine for subtraction is closely related to Take Ten. Display Nifty Nine: Beads on the interactive whiteboard. Point out the "– 9" in each problem.

2. Use the first problem, 12 – 9, as an example. Say: *I see that 9 is the subtrahend. Since 9 is very close to 10, I'll first think of what happens if we take 10 away. We only need to remove the tens place from the minuend, so that leaves us with 2. Now, since 10 is really one more than 9, the second step is to add one more to that answer, which means 2 goes up to 3. Now that I've figured out the answer in my head, I can double check by using beads as counters.*

3. Drag 12 counters onto the necklace. (Note that the beads are infinitely cloned.) Then drag 9 away. Count the remaining beads, then write "3" as the answer to the first problem.

4. Invite volunteers to follow your lead and think aloud as they work through the remaining problems on the board.

5. Click on the check boxes to confirm students' answers.

More Practice

On the second page of Nifty Nine: Beads, students can have more practice with the Nifty Nine strategy. Have them check their answers by using the beads on the interactive whiteboard.

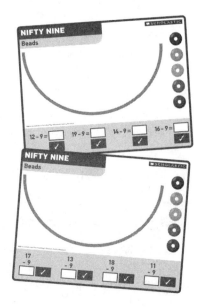

Nifty Nine: Pockets

Ready . . . Review the Activity

Students practice subtracting 9 by moving pennies into pockets on the interactive whiteboard.

Set . . . Explain the Strategy

An easy way to solve subtraction problems with 9 as the subtrahend is to start with the Take Ten strategy, then move up one to find the difference.

Go . . . Practice the Strategy

1. Review the Nifty Nine strategy and note how similar it is to the Take Ten strategy. Remind students that to subtract 9 from another number, they should first imagine taking 10 away from the number, then count up one to get to the final answer.

2. Display Nifty Nine: Pockets on the interactive whiteboard. Work through the first problem using the strategy. Say: *With 16 – 9, I know that if I were taking 10 away, I would end up with 6. But since 10 is one more than 9, I'm going to add one more to 6. So the final answer is 7. That's how the Nifty Nine strategy works.*

3. Next, model how to check the answer by manipulating counters. Point out the two numbers in the problem. Say: *We know that there are a total of 16 pennies for this problem and we want to see how many pennies is that away from 9.* Explain that 16 – 9 = ___ is the same as 9 + ___ = 16. Continue explaining: *Let's start by moving 9 pennies into the first pocket on the board. Then we'll count up to 16 to figure out what the missing addend is in 9 + ___ = 16.* Count as you move pennies into the second pocket: *10, 11, 12, 13, 14, 15, 16.* Ask students how many pennies are in that pocket. *(7)* Write "7" next the first problem.

4. Have students solve the remaining problems by using the Nifty Nine strategy and then dragging pennies into pockets for a visual check.

5. Ask students to write the differences. Finish by clicking on the check boxes to confirm answers together.

More Practice

Invite students to continue practicing the Nifty Nine strategy on the second page of Nifty Nine: Pockets. Explain that as they work, they're using another strategy called Think Addition, because when they figure out how many pennies should go in the second problem, they're also thinking about an addition problem with a missing addend.

MATH TIP:
RTI and Progress Monitoring

Keep track of how much students have mastered their facts by reviewing what they've learned at the end of a lesson as well as from previous lessons. Alternate between informal oral review and written review in the form of independent practice, as well as math journals. As you monitor students' progress in addition and subtraction, prepare your lessons so that you differentiate your instruction. You may wish to ask only a few students to use the More Practice boards with you, while the rest of the class works independently or rotates to centers.

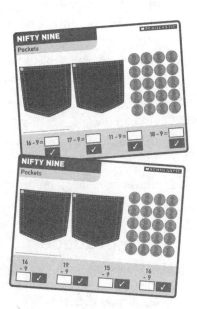

Think Addition: Block Towers

Ready . . . Review the Activity

By building with on-screen blocks, students will see how they can use addition to solve subtraction problems.

Set . . . Explain the Strategy

The Think Addition strategy for subtraction is similar to counting up in addition. This strategy helps students realize how closely connected the operations of addition and subtraction are. Rather than looking at a subtraction problem to find the difference, students reverse their thinking and ask themselves how many more they need to add or count up.

Go . . . Practice the Strategy

1. Display Think Addition: Block Towers on the interactive whiteboard. Ask students what kind of operation they see in each of the problems. (*Subtraction*) Explain that you see the minus symbol, too, but you're now going to show them a strategy that uses addition to solve the subtraction problems on the board.

2. Begin with the first problem: 12 − 7. Say: *I know that I've got to get from 7 to 12 in order to find the solution. I'll think of what I would need to add to 7 to arrive at 12. I can either remember my addition fact, 7 + ___ = 12, or I can try counting up from 7. Let's count up together after 7: 8, 9, 10, 11, 12. We counted up five times, so the answer is 5.*

3. Next, demonstrate the problem using block towers. Explain that you'll build one tower using two different color blocks. Drag seven green blocks and stack them vertically. Then add one orange block at a time, counting up as you do until you reach 12. Say: *We start with 7, and now here's 8, 9, 10, 11, and one more makes 12.* Then count how many orange blocks there are, pointing out that you came up with the same answer. Write "5" next to the first problem.

4. Invite students to come up to the board and make a tall, two-colored tower for each problem. Ask them to count up as they drag the blocks. Then have them count how many blocks they added to find the answer.

5. Finish by clicking on the check boxes to confirm students' answers.

More Practice

Give students extra practice using addition to solve subtraction problems on the second page of Think Addition: Block Towers on the interactive whiteboard.

TECH TIP:
SMART Recorder

Printing out activities isn't the only way to save them for students who have missed the lesson or need additional help. Launch the SMART Recorder to see a small recording window. Click the record button to begin, and then everything you do on the screen will be recorded. You can even add audio and video as you record. After you've finished modeling one problem or doing whatever steps you want recorded, click the stop button. You can then save your recording to your computer and later burn it to a CD to send home with your students.

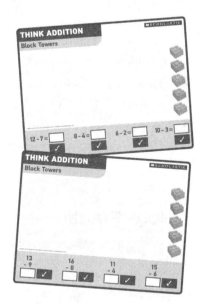

Think Addition: Beads

Ready ... Review the Activity

Students practice using addition to solve subtraction problems by moving colorful beads across the interactive whiteboard to help them visualize this strategy.

Set ... Explain the Strategy

Students think of related addition facts to solve subtraction problems.

Go ... Practice the Strategy

1. Open a blank page on the interactive whiteboard and write the following problems: "2 + ___ = 6" and "4 + ___ = 9." Have students solve the problems, and then ask how they got the answers.

2. Explain that one way to find missing addends in addition problems is by using subtraction. So, 2 + ___ = 6 turns into 6 – 2 = 4, and 4 + ___ = 9 becomes 9 – 4 = 5. Point out that these facts are in the same family.

3. Tell students that they're going to use what they know about addition to solve subtraction problems, and that they'll use beads to check their answers. Display Think Addition: Beads on the interactive whiteboard.

4. Use the first problem, 9 – 6, to demonstrate. Say: *I know that I can turn this subtraction problem into an addition problem. It becomes 6 + ___ = 9.* To demonstrate the problem, move six purple beads to the center of the screen, as if making a necklace. Ask: *How many more beads do we need to get 9?* Count aloud as you add three green beads to the necklace: *7, 8, 9.* Check by counting how many beads you've added. Finish by reading aloud the problem after you've written the answer: *9 – 6 = 3.* Point out that this is the same as 6 + 3 = 9.

5. Invite students to come up to the board to solve the other problems, following the steps you showed. Suggest that they first convert the subtraction problem to an addition problem with a missing addend. Then they can choose a different color bead for each addend.

6. Click on the check boxes to confirm students' answers together.

More Practice

Offer students more opportunity to practice doing subtraction by using addition. Invite them to create more virtual bead necklaces on the second page of Think Addition: Beads on the interactive whiteboard.

MATH TIP:
Real-Life Problems

Connect the math concepts to scenarios students encounter in their lives. Explain how thinking about addition and subtraction together can help solve problems, such as planning the beads to fit on a necklace. For example, give a story problem such as: *Mateo wants to make a blue and red necklace that has ten beads in all. He has four blue beads. How many red beads does he need?* Show students how to set up the problem in both subtraction and addition. You can then challenge students to relate these problems to money. An extension problem for the sample could be: *At the store, ten beads cost $1. You pay with a $5 bill. How much money will you get back?*

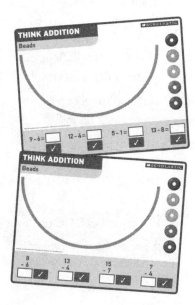

Think Addition: Pockets

Using the pennies and pockets activity, students show how parts of a problem make the whole.

Set . . . Explain the Strategy

When students stop to remember the connection between subtraction and addition, they can solve any problem. To do this, they simply reverse the operation so that they solve for the missing addend rather than find the difference.

Go . . . Practice the Strategy

1. Write a few subtraction problems on the blank board. Practice converting subtraction problems into addition problems with missing addends. For example, show students how to turn $2 - 1 = \_\_\_$ into $1 + \_\_\_ = 2$ and $7 - 5 = \_\_\_$ into $5 + \_\_\_ = 7$.

2. Display Think Addition: Pockets on the interactive whiteboard. Point out that subtraction problems can be made easy when you think of them as addition problems.

3. Model with the first problem: $6 - 3$. Explain that you can change the problem into addition by taking the total number, 6, and making it the sum. Then take the subtrahend and turn it into an addend. The next step is to then figure out what is the missing addend. Write $3 + \_\_\_ = 6$ under the first problem.

4. Show students how to use pennies to stand for the parts of the problem. Count and drag three pennies into the first pocket. Then drag additional pennies to the other pocket, counting up aloud after 3: *4, 5, 6.* Have students note that in the second pocket, there are now three pennies, which is the answer. Write "3" in two places—as the difference in the subtraction problem on the board and as the addend on the blank line in the addition problem you wrote.

5. Have volunteers solve the other problems in the same manner, and then check their answers together.

TECH TIP: SMART Keyboard

Access a keyboard by touching the keyboard icon on the front tray of the SMART Board. Without having to return to your computer, you can add text to the screen by typing. Use the on-screen keyboard to start a lesson with a story problem for students to read or to label problems with the strategies for solving them.

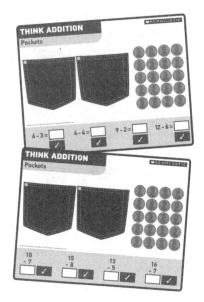

More Practice

Display the second page of Think Addition: Pockets on the interactive whiteboard to have students continue practicing how to visualize subtraction problems as addition problems. Check their answers as a group.

Subtraction Template: Number Line

Ready ... Review the Activity

Students can use a number line on the interactive whiteboard to help them solve subtraction problems by "hopping backward."

Set ... Explain the Strategy

Feel free to choose any of the subtraction strategies using the number line for further practice. Or write a random assortment of subtraction problems and have students choose which strategy will best help them.

Go ... Practice the Strategy

1. Display the Subtraction Template: Number Line on the interactive whiteboard and write a set of problems that involve subtraction facts for 0 to 10.

2. Review the strategy you want students to use. If students need a refresher, show them how to use either the pointer or the pen to hop back each tick mark on the number line.

3. Invite volunteers to solve the problems on the board, using the number line to check their answers.

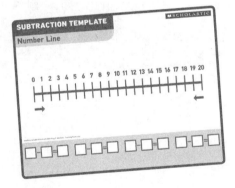

MATH TIP:
Problem-Solver Pairs

Guide students to use self-monitoring as they practice solving subtraction problems on the SMART Board with a partner. Allow pairs to revisit an activity that you have already introduced to the whole class or a small group. Let one student be the problem solver and the other be the listener. The problem solver works through the steps modeled to solve each problem, while the listener weighs in with any suggestions. Then have the students switch roles. When a pair has had time to practice, you may invite them to lead an activity together for a larger group.

More Practice

Follow up by clearing the board and writing more problems. Talk about how to solve the new set of problems, and then give students more hands-on practice to find the differences.

Subtraction Template: Block Towers

Ready... Review the Activity

Building with blocks gives students a visual reference for solving subtraction problems. They can see quantities as they use different strategies to find solutions.

Set... Explain the Strategy

Decide on which strategy you would like students to focus on as they work through various subtraction problems.

Go... Practice the Strategy

1. Before you display Subtraction Template: Block Towers, think about whether you want to give students problems that all have the same subtrahend or the same minuend, or a mix of problems.

2. Review the steps of the strategy you want students to follow. You may want them to talk through a strategy first or have them go straight to the blocks to help them solve the problems.

3. Go over their answers together as a class.

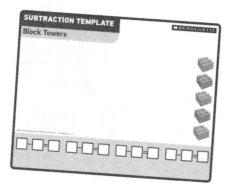

MATH TIP:
RTI and Hands-on Learning

Some students may benefit from having printed copies of the activity you are doing on the interactive whiteboard, as well as manipulatives that match the kind that appear on the board. Encourage students to work with counters on their desks as you model on the board. By connecting the interactive whiteboard, paper, and manipulatives, you can help make abstract learning more concrete.

More Practice

Erase the problems on the board, and write up another set of problems. Ask volunteers to think of strategies to practice and problems to solve using those strategies. Vary the activity by having students build vertical towers or lay out the blocks horizontally in a row.

Subtraction Template: Beads

Ready . . . Review the Activity

Use this template screen as a setup for subtraction practice using beads as counters.

Set . . . Explain the Strategy

Review any of the subtraction strategies you taught earlier with this template.

Go . . . Practice the Strategy

1. Write a set of subtraction problems on the board for Subtraction Template: Beads.

2. Talk about what you want students to think about as they work on this activity, emphasizing the strategy or strategies you want them to use.

3. Choose one student or a small group of students to lead the steps toward solving the problem, encouraging them to use the beads to show their work. Finish by checking their answers together with the class.

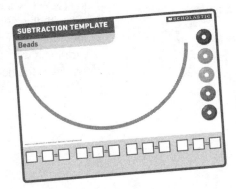

More Practice

Invite student volunteers to write subtraction problems for peers. Encourage them to think of a strategy to practice and a number of problems that serve as examples. Have them call up classmates to solve the problems and to use beads to work through the solution. Review answers as a group.

MATH TIP:
Place-Value Board

Create place-value boards to help students with strategies like Take Ten. For each small group of students, make a T-chart with the left half made of blue construction paper and the right half kept white. Ask the students to "read" the board. When they respond that nothing is on the board, ask what the number word is for "nothing." *(Zero)* Explain that they can read the blank board as "zero." Then give each group of students a set of 20 interlocking cubes. Ask students to add one cube to the ones column (the right side of the board). Explain that when there's a zero in the tens column, we don't have to say it. With one cube in the ones column, the board now reads as "one." Have students continue adding cubes to the ones column—stopping to read the board after each cube is added—until they get to 9. When they get to 10, point out that they need to make a change. They should snap the 10 cubes together and put it into the tens column (the blue left side) as one set of tens, leaving the ones column empty. Explain that one tens and zero ones is read as "10." Have students continue adding cubes and reading their boards until they get to 19.

Subtraction Template: Pockets

Ready ... Review the Activity

Students practice moving pennies into pockets to help them solve subtraction problems.

Set ... Explain the Strategy

Use any of the subtraction strategies for this activity, depending on your preferences and the needs of your students.

Go ... Practice the Strategy

1. After you've decided on the types of subtraction problems your students could use more practice with, set up the interactive whiteboard by writing problems on the Subtraction Template: Pockets file.

2. Display Subtraction Template: Pockets. Discuss how you want students to solve the problems on the board, explaining whether you want them to state the strategy they are using and think aloud as they use it, or whether they can go directly to using the pennies and pockets on the board.

3. Invite students to solve the problems on the board, using the pennies and pockets as manipulatives. Check their answers together.

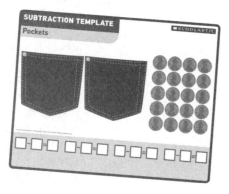

MATH TIP:
More Money

As students master solving addition and subtraction problems with pennies, give them the added challenge of using other coins. Provide story problems and sets of pennies, nickels, dimes, and quarters. Ask students to practice moving about real coins on their desks or putting them in physical pockets. You can support their understanding by creating new SMART Notebook lessons that involve different coins. After your students have had practice moving pennies between pockets on the interactive whiteboard, as they did with this set of activities, they can try more challenging problems with on-screen counters that looks like nickels, dimes, and quarters.

More Practice

Erase the board and start afresh. Give extra practice with either the same or another strategy. Or write problems that call for a variety of strategies. Have students solve the subtraction problems and then check their answers.